Friendship
101

Quizzes and Questions

For all the readers and *their* friends 4-ever.

—J.H.

For Cami, Diann, and Mylisa,
who've taught me all about friendship.

—T.M.

ISBN 0-439-86646-4
Text copyright © 2006 Scholastic Inc.
Illustrations copyright © 2006 Scholastic Inc.

12 11 10 9 8 7 6 5 4   8 9 10 11/0

Printed in the U.S.A.
First printing, October 2006
Book design by Carla Siegel

Friends 4 Ever

Friendship 101

Quizzes and Questions

by Jo Hurley
Illustrated by Taia Morley

Scholastic Inc.
New York   Toronto   London   Auckland   Sydney
Mexico City   New Delhi   Hong Kong   Buenos Aires

Rachel

Name: Rachel

Nickname: Red

Style: Artsy

Hobbies: Crafts, music, acting

Favorite Place: Theater (onstage!)

Favorite Sport: Swimming

Favorite Snack: Granola and yogurt

Hidden Talent: Always optimistic

Sometimes Known As: Drama Queen

Sam

Name: Samantha

Nickname: Sam

Style: Casual

Hobbies: Hiking, biking

Favorite Place: The gym

Favorite Sport: Soccer, skiing, sailing

Favorite Snack: Energy bar

Hidden Talent: Making people laugh

Sometimes Known As: The Athlete

JESSIE

Name: Jessica

Nickname: Jessie

Style: Girly

Hobbies: Reading, writing, babysitting

Favorite Place: The library

Favorite Sport: Tennis

Favorite Snack: Corn chips

Hidden Talent: Great Listener

Sometimes Known As: The Great Brain

Name: Elizabeth

Nickname: Libby

Style: Glam

Hobbies: Volunteering, cooking

Favorite Place: Anywhere with lots of people

Favorite Sport: Dance

Favorite Snack: Fruit salad

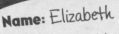

Hidden Talent: Never at a loss for words

Sometimes Known As: Party Girl

Libby

To Quiz or Not to Quiz?

If you're like us, you dread pop quizzes in school. Ugh. There *are* some quizzes, however, that are fun to take—anytime, anywhere. This is a book of quizzes and questions all about friendship. We like to call it *Friendship 101*.

The quizzes and questions in this book are destined to be . . .

a) Another cool way to see how alike you and your friends are.

b) Fun games to play at your next slumber party.

c) A true measure of how you think, what you feel, and what you love to do.

d) All of the above—and soooo much MORE!

Am I a Prima Princess or a Pack Rat? I just have to know! Don't you?

Taking quizzes gets me quick info on all my BFFs. I can learn something brand new about them!

If you ask the right question . . . you will get a great answer. Um . . . now I just need the list of questions.

TAKING QUIZZES MAKES ME FEEL SUPERSMART AND GIVES ME MY PRECISE Q^2, WHICH IS SHORT FOR QUIZ-Q, WHICH IS THE NEXT BEST THING TO MY IQ. GOT IT?

How True Blue Is Your Friend?

How can you tell when a friend is really going to be there for you? Learn how to read the signs. Take this colorful quiz and find out.

1 **When you've got the flu, your friend . . .**

a) Makes you chicken soup and a homemade card.

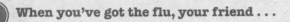

b) Sends you a Get Well Soon e-card.

c) Doesn't call or come over until she knows you're feeling better. She doesn't want to catch your germs.

2 **When your friend calls your house and your mom answers, your friend says . . .**

a) "Hello, Mrs. Smith. How are you? Is Mary home?"

b) "Hey. Is Mary there?"

c) "Yo! Put Mary on the phone."

3 You just had a huge fight with your mom. As you talk about it, your friend . . .

a) Listens for hours until you feel better.

b) Says she's sorry but wants to talk about other stuff, too.

c) Changes the subject.

4 You haven't finished prepping and your test is next period! Your friend . . .

a) Lets you read her notes even if she hasn't finished studying.

b) Helps you review the main points of the test.

c) Shrugs and wishes you luck.

5 There's a huge party coming up. When you ask a friend for fashion advice, she . . .

a) Lends you her favorite sweater.

b) Offers to go shopping together.

c) Suggests you wear whatever you have on. What's the big deal, anyway?

6 You and a friend are in a school play together. When you forget your lines, your friend . . .

- a) Steps in with a line to cover your mistake so no one knows you goofed.

- b) Whispers your line from offstage to help you out.

- c) Cracks up.

7 Someone at school makes a joke at your expense. Your friend, who is also standing there . . .

- a) Sticks up for you with a great comment of her own.

- b) Tells you to ignore the joker and walk away.

- c) Stands there and says nothing until the joker walks away.

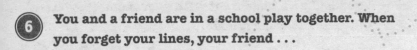

Ha Ha!

Ha Ha!

Ha Ha!

Ha Ha!

Ha Ha!

Ha Ha!

Your TRUE BLUE Score

If you picked mostly *A*s, you're TURQUOISE BLUE.
Your friendship is all about deep feelings and total loyalty. Your friend believes in sticking by you through bad times and good times—no matter what. You're lucky to have a friend like her!

If you picked mostly *B*s, you're NEON BLUE.
Your friend is bright and cheery most of the time, but sometimes your friendship can blaze hot and then cold. You can't be sure that your friend will always understand what you need, even though she may have the best intentions. But if you tell her how you feel, usually she will be there for you.

If you picked mostly *C*s, you're POWDER BLUE.
Like powder blue, your friendship isn't big on bright color or bold statements. In fact, this friend doesn't really seem to understand when you need her most. Think about how much you invest in this friendship. You can have a good time together, but don't expect much support. Your friend probably has something else on her mind.

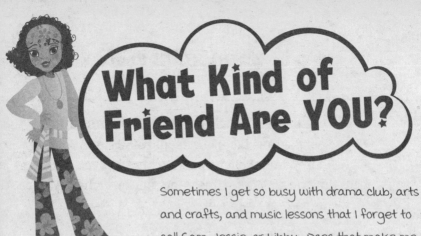

What Kind of Friend Are YOU?

Sometimes I get so busy with drama club, arts and crafts, and music lessons that I forget to call Sam, Jessie, or Libby. Does that make me a bad friend? What kind of a friend are you? Take this quiz to find out.

1 **There's a new girl at school. You and your friend both like her a lot, so you . . .**

a) Invite the new girl to join you and your friend after school to go shopping together.

b) Ask the new girl to sit with you and your friend at lunch.

c) Call the new girl and invite her over to your house alone.

2 **You forgot a good friend's birthday. What do you do now?**

a) Immediately run out and get her a funny card and her favorite candy bar—with a promise to make it up to her.

b) Apologize and sing "Happy Birthday" over the phone in your loudest voice.

c) Say "whoopsie" and tell her you'll do something about it later.

3   **Oh, no! Your friend was invited to a cool class party and you weren't. What now?**

a) Forget about it. It's only one party—and your friend probably won't stay very long without you, anyhow.

b) Ask your friend if the two of you can go together—even without an invite for you.

c) Beg your friend to boycott the party in protest.

4   **A friend wants to borrow your brand-new sweater. You haven't even worn it yet. What do you say?**

a) "Okay, you can wear it. I know you'll take good care of it."

b) "Can I lend you something else instead?"

c) "No way! I can't loan you something I just got!"

5 **Can you always be honest with your friend?**

a) Almost all the time—except when it might hurt someone's feelings.

b) Of course you can. Honesty is the best policy no matter what.

c) Nah. It's better to keep my mouth shut.

6 **You and your BFF have a celebrity sighting of your favorite actor of all time. Your friend starts talking to him. Now what?**

a) You let your friend do all the talking. Eventually he'll have to talk to you, too.

b) You try to get a word in edgewise, making jokes to get him to laugh and notice you.

c) You completely cut off your friend's conversation and start one of your own.

7 **Your BFF just got mad at you for no reason. Now you need to . . .**

a) Find out what's bugging her.

b) Shout, "Stop that!" and pout it out.

c) Ignore her until she realizes she's been mean to you.

8 **The most important thing about friendship is . . .**

a) The shared experiences.

b) Knowing someone's secrets.

c) Having as many pals as possible.

9 **When two of your friends have a fight, you usually . . .**

a) Step in to mediate the argument.

b) Cover your eyes and scream, "Nooooooooo! Stop now!"

c) Pretend as if you never heard.

10 **How do you greet your friends?**

    a) "Hi! It's so good to see you!"

    b) "Whassup?"

    c) Don't say anything. Just raise a hand as if to say, "Hey, there."

11 **How would your friends describe you?**

    a) At home in large and small crowds.

    b) At ease with a very small group of people.

    c) A little bit of a loner.

12 **Your friend did something really embarrassing. Now you must . . .**

    a) Solemnly promise never to speak about the incident again.

    b) Make a joke about it so she feels better.

    c) Pretend that you don't know her. You don't want to be humiliated, too!

Your FRIENDSHIP Score

If you picked mostly *A*s, you're UP FOR ANYTHING.
You're a wild and crazy friend who's always ready to go—to the movies, to the mall, wherever the action is! Just don't forget to let your friends know what you need, too. A good friendship is all about sharing and understanding.

If you picked mostly *B*s, you're EMOTIONAL.
You usually lend a helping hand or try to get involved, but sometimes situations overwhelm you. Try to see things from your friend's point of view. Sometimes your job as a good friend is to listen—and just be there.

If you picked mostly *C*s, you're AFRAID TO GET INVOLVED.
Although you consider yourself a good friend, you sometimes back away from conflict—when you could be sticking around to help. Don't be afraid to stick your neck out for your friend. Chances are that there will come a moment when you need help—and she'll be there for you, too.

TWO Close for Comfort?

You're good friends, but is there such a thing as too close for comfort? Does your friend do everything you do? Is your BFF really your twin? Check off the items that apply to you and your friend. Then total up the number you checked off. Look at page 19 to see how you scored.

My Friend and I . . .

☐ Like the same people in school.

☐ Borrow each other's shoes.

☐ Dislike the same people in school.

☐ Take a lot of the same classes.

☐ Play the same sports.

☐ Finish each other's sentences.

☐ Wear the same colors a lot.

☐ Wear our hair the same way.

☐ Have the same middle name.

☐ Laugh at the same kind of jokes.

☐ Have the same first name.

☐ Go on family vacations together.

☐ Eat the same lunch in the cafeteria.

☐ Listen to the same music.

☐ Have the same kind of pet.

I LOOKED UP SOME COOL "TWIN-FO" ON THE INTERNET. LIKE. . . ARE YOU AND YOUR FRIEND BOTH GEMINIS? THAT'S THE ZODIAC SIGN OF TWINS. DID YOU KNOW THAT THE WORD TWIN COMES FROM THE GERMAN WORD TWINE, WHICH MEANS "TWO TOGETHER"? AND EVERY YEAR TWINS TRAVEL TO TWINSBURG, OHIO, FOR TWIN DAY, THE LARGEST GATHERING OF TWINS IN THE UNITED STATES. WHEW. THAT'S ONE WAY TO DOUBLE THE FUN, RIGHT?

Your TWIN Score

If you checked off . . .

1–4 You don't seem to have that much "twin" common after all. Your friend is less like your mirror image and more like your flip side. But that keeps things interesting.

5–9 Wow! You two have sooo many things in common. You share similar likes and dislikes—and you can probably read each other's minds sometimes. How cool is that? But always remember: Keeping your individuality within a friendship is important.

10–14 Beware: twin alert! You two are so much alike that people think you're practically attached at the hip. But here's a suggestion: Try new things and find the quirks and ideas that set you apart. Sometimes it's our differences that make us closer and more interesting to one another.

15 Okay. Forget twins. You are the *exact* same person. How do you tell each other apart?

Beauty Is in the of the Beholder

Beauty is more than skin deep. I totally love being glam, but beautiful is what's on the inside, too.

Olympic athletes are beautiful. Winning a gold medal has to be the most beautiful thing of all.

A NEWBORN BABY WITH PINK SKIN AND CHUBBY CHEEKS! I REMEMBER THE DAY MY LITTLE BROTHER WAS BORN. I THOUGHT HE WAS THE MOST BEAUTIFUL THING I HAD EVER SEEN.

I like long, curly hair. mine gets even curlier when it rains, and I think it looks and feels beautiful.

What's Your BEAUTY MARK?

What's BEAUTIFUL to YOU? Here are some quick quizzes on beauty—and everything that goes with it.

1 **The best shampoo for me smells like . . .**

    a) Nothing. I prefer unscented.

    b) Bubble gum or chocolate.

    c) Lavender or peppermint.

    d) Roses.

2 **The best lotion for me would be . . .**

    a) Whatever's on sale.

    b) Whatever brand the stars use.

    c) Aloe gel right from the plant.

    d) Perfumed cold cream from Mom's dresser.

3 **The best kind of makeup for me would be . . .**

    a) Earth tones.

    b) Pastel glitter all the time.

    c) Anything, as long as it's not tested on animals.

    d) Whatever Mom lets me wear.

4 Where do you keep your beauty products?

a) In a little case on my dresser.

b) In my backpack with my cell phone.

c) In my pocket.

d) On the bathroom counter.

5 You like this kind of jewelry the best . . .

a) Silver rings and bangles.

b) Trendy charm bracelets and whatever else pop stars are wearing.

c) Dangling bead earrings.

d) Grandma's vintage pearl necklace.

6 This hairstyle makes you stand out in a crowd . . .

a) No muss, no fuss, au natural.

b) Spiky bangs with highlights.

c) Long and curly.

d) Updo with pretty barrettes.

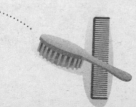

BEAUTY MARK Answers

....

Mostly *As*? You're ALL NATURAL.

You opt for simple beauty products and fashion statements. You have an easygoing way about you. Best of
all: You're low maintenance. You'd be just as comfort-
able using a drugstore lotion as you would be using a
jar of cream from some fancy shop.

....

Mostly *Bs*? You're TRENDY COOL.

You read all the latest gossip and fashion magazines in
search of the hottest new trends in beauty. Although
you probably don't wear a ton of makeup, you know
about all the different brands. You're off-the-charts cool
when it comes to beauty stuff.

....

Mostly *Cs*? You're a HIPPIE CHICK.

You like laid-back, bohemian beauty. You love long hair,
loose clothes, and lots of jewelry on your ears, fingers,
and even toes.

....

Mostly *Ds*? You're FORMAL.

You take a lot of your beauty cues from Mom, which is
good because then you can borrow all of her stuff! You
wear jewelry handed down in your family and go for
simple, conservative styles.

....

Mini-Quiz:
How Often Do You Use These Items?

Rate your usage on a scale from 1 to 5 as follows:

1 = Never use it
2 = Once or twice
3 = Sometimes just for fun
4 = For dances, parties, and dressing up
5 = All the time

	5	4	3	2	1
1. Blusher	5	4	3	2	1
2. Mascara	5	4	3	2	1
3. Lip gloss	5	4	3	2	1
4. Lipstick	5	4	3	2	1
5. Body glitter	5	4	3	2	1
6. Nail polish	5	4	3	2	1
7. Cover-up	5	4	3	2	1
8. Hair gel or hair spray	5	4	3	2	1
9. Perfume	5	4	3	2	1
10. Eye shadow	5	4	3	2	1
11. Curling iron or curlers	5	4	3	2	1
12. Jewelry	5	4	3	2	1

Mostly 1s:
Makeup and perfume don't really matter to you.

Mostly 2s:
Sometimes you add a little color, just for fun makeovers with friends.

Mostly 3s:
You get decked out for every special occasion—for sure.

Mostly 4s:
You would die without your strawberry lip gloss.

Mostly 5s:
Your middle name is "MMUN, aka Make Me Up NOW."

Hey, remember that the natural look is just fine. No one looks like a model all the time. Not even models!

Closet 101: What Your Clothes Say About You

Check off all of the clothes and other items you have (or wish you had) in your bedroom. Then tally up the answers. Which column has the most checks?

Closet A
- Short, flouncy skirts
- Stockings with little hearts and flowers
- Cute shrug sweater with fake-fur collar
- Ballet flats with bows

Closet B
- Grandma's hand-knit sweater
- Worn-in jeans piled on your bedroom floor
- Soft, wrinkled T-shirts (stolen from your brother's closet)
- Faded corduroy jacket with patches

TTYL

Closet C
- A hipster tee advertised in a fashion magazine
- Low-rise denim jeans
- Rows of silver bangles and a toe ring
- Designer platform shoes

Closet 101 Scores

Closet A = PRIMA PRINCESS.

You need a tiara, girlfriend! Always dressing in the pink makes you a prima princess indeed. Your super spread of clothes and shoes is like cotton candy and candy canes—just sweeeeeet.

Closet B = PACK RAT.

You never throw anything out. Recycling outfits can be cool as long as you don't wear stuff with too many holes or rips, right? But vintage rocks!

Closet C = Fashionista.

If it isn't featured on the cover of the hottest tween 'zine, then it just isn't cool enough to be in your fashion ensemble. You're a style-setter in your circle of friends.

Pssst! If you checked off everything or had an even mix of all three columns, you belong in another category altogether: THE RACHEL CLOSET, named after our Friend 4-Ever Rachel, who successfully mixes all three styles to come up with a totally unique Renaissance-girl look. After all, the best style is the one you make up as you go along!

This or That?

TAKE THE TEST ON YOUR OWN. THEN TEST A FRIEND.
HOW MANY OF YOUR ANSWERS ARE THE SAME?

Fortune Cookies **OR** Chocolate chip cookies

Blue **OR** Red · Breakfast **OR** Lunch · Radio **OR** iPod

Road trip **OR** Plane ride · Flip-flops **OR** Heels

 Dogs **OR** Cats · Vitamin water **OR** Tap water

Surf **OR** Ski · Bath **OR** Shower · IM **OR** Phone call

T-shirt **OR** Nightgown · French fries **OR** Carrot sticks

Jeans **OR** Cords · Book **OR** Movie · Zoo **OR** Museum

Wool blanket **OR** Puffy comforter · Little purse **OR** Little backpack

Lemons **OR** Limes · Manicure **OR** Pedicure

Rave About Your FAVES!

(Who Knows What You Might Reveal?)

1 **Which of these candy bars is your favorite?**

    a) Heath Bar

    b) Snickers

    c) Hershey's Milk Chocolate Bar

2 **Which of these is your favorite pizza topping?**

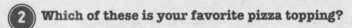

    a) Pineapple

    b) Pepperoni

    c) Plain cheese

3 **Which of these flowers would you want in a bouquet?**

    a) Exotic lily

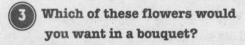

    b) Rose

    c) Daisy

4 **Which of these sports do you like the best?**

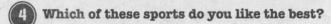

    a) Extreme snowboarding

    b) Baseball

    c) Tennis

5 Which of these ice-cream flavors is your favorite?

    a) Chunky peanut butter brittle fudge ripple

    b) Mint chip

    c) French vanilla

6 Which of these breakfast cereals would you eat the most?

    a) Granola with dried cranberries

    b) Cinnamon Toast Crunch

    c) Cornflakes

7 Which of these symbols feels most like you?

    a) Your astrological sign

    b) Smiley face

    c) Peace sign

8 Which of these drinks do you like the best?

    a) Green-tea lemonade

    b) Diet soda

    c) Chocolate milk

9 Which of these shoes would you be the most likely to buy?

    a) Flip-flips with colored crystals

    b) Platforms

    c) Sneakers

10 **Which potato chip flavor do you love?**

    a) Salt and vinegar

    b) Honey barbecue

    c) Plain

11 **Which of these Pooh characters is the most like you?**

    a) Tigger

    b) Pooh

    c) Eeyore

12 **Which of these sandwiches do you like the best?**

    a) Roast chicken panini

    b) Ham and cheese

    c) Peanut butter and jelly

· · · · · · · · · · · · · · · · **Your Score: FAVES** · · · · · · · · · · · · · · · · · · ·

Mostly *A*s
You Dare to Be Different. In the future, you might end up being a rock star, astronaut, politician, chef, or journalist.

Mostly *B*s
You Go with the Crowd. In the future, you might end up being a teacher, dancer, police officer, doctor, or firefighter.

Mostly *C*s
You Keep a Low Profile. In the future, you might end up being a Web designer, accountant, or psychologist.

A Room of One's Own—Totally

There are TWO ways to answer these questions!

version #1:

Fill in the blanks on page 32, then have your friend fill in the same answers on page 33. See how many of your answers match.

version #2:

Fill in the blanks on page 32 with the answers you think your friend will give. Then ask her the questions aloud. How close did you come to your friend's actual answers? Have your friend use page 33 to write in answers she thinks you will give. How does she score?

What's on the floor of your closet? _____

What's on the top of your dresser? _____

What colors are on your walls? _____

If you could buy a new piece of furniture, what would it be? _____

What's hanging on your windows? _____

Do you have a television or computer in your room? _____

What's on the floor? _____

Do you have art on the walls? _____

What photos are on your wall or bulletin board? _____

What kind of lamp do you use to read? _____

Is there a ceiling fan in your room? _____

What's on the back of your bedroom door? _____

What's on the floor of your closet? _____

What's on the top of your dresser? _____

What colors are on your walls? _____

If you could buy a new piece of furniture, what would it be? _____

What's hanging on your windows? _____

Do you have a television or computer in your room? _____

What's on the floor? _____

Do you have art on the walls? _____

What photos are on your wall or bulletin board? _____

What kind of lamp do you use to read? _____

Is there a ceiling fan in your room? _____

What's on the back of your bedroom door? _____

Figure Your SPACE OUT

(With the Help of Your Friends, of Course)

Frame stuff. Put old and new photos into an oversized collage and frame it over your bed. If your friends help to design it, have everyone sign and scribble a secret message somewhere on the picture. I just looooove making crafts!

Pick a theme you love. Choose a theme like "By the Sea." Fill a fishbowl with seashells and paint the walls sea green with colored fish swimming everywhere.

Or, make your theme "Moonbeams." Put glow-in-the-dark stars on the ceiling. Personally, I love the "Reading Room" theme. Put up floor-to-ceiling bookshelves for all your favorite reads.

Discover chalkboard paint. Why settle for plain old paint when you can paint a chalkboard on the back of your closet door? A great alternative to a notepad, chalkboard paint converts any wall or door into a writing surface. Plus, you can work out plays for the next big sports event. Bonus!

Here's a scent-sational idea. Have your mom get lavender or floral potpourri and put some in a dish. It will transform your room with its sweet smell. I also love incense, fresh flowers, and other stuff like that. It's girly and glam.

What Kind of Room Makeover Do You Need?

Check off each item that reflects your room the best . . . and discover what kind of room makeover you need most. Good Luck!

There are pillows all over the bed—but the colors don't coordinate.

The latest photograph on your mirror was taken in first grade.

Which pile has dirty laundry and which pile has clean clothes?

Oh, no! You can't find a bare spot of carpet to walk on your bedroom floor.

On the cool chair in the corner is a pile of stuffed animals from when you were five.

Your walls are painted boring gray and there's no art anywhere.

Where's the desk? You can't find your cell phone charger under all those old magazines.

The lamps have plain shades and the dresser has plain knobs.

You still have your "blankie" from childhood stuffed under your pillow.

Now match the shapes you picked most with the corresponding letter and read about your makeover style on the next page.

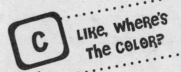
A Pick up my mess — pronto!

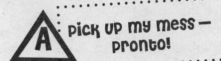
C Like, where's the color?

B Funkier decor, please!

Here's the deal. Your picks say sooo much about your style.
But most important, they clue me in to what you need to do first
in a room redo. I consider myself Queen of Room Redesign, so . . .
pay close attention!

If you ended up with the message . . .

PICK UP MY MESS — PRONTO!

You need to get better organized. That means going through all those papers and junk before they take over! Add fun storage boxes or bins. Put up a bulletin board for loose notes and photos. Have your parents help you install a shelving system in and out of your closet. Imagine what it'll be like once you know where everything is!

FUNKIER DECOR, PLEASE!

Your room is neat and you know where all your stuff is. But that Pooh rug and alphabet mirror don't really work anymore. It's time for a more grown-up look. Clear up clutter with funky oversize baskets. Get new sheets with geometric designs or bright colors. Then add pillows, a funky chair, or a framed art poster.

LIKE, WHERE'S THE COLOR?

It's time to spice up those plain white or beige walls and brighten up your space. Use a vibrant, rich color scheme. Why not try deep purples or loud oranges? Go for something bold. Color combinations like pink and gold will make your space extra special. Find fabrics, frames, and shades that coordinate. Your room will sparkle in no time!

Do the Right Thing?

Sometimes it's tough to do the right thing. But being true to your friends and to yourself will help your relationships grow. Take this quiz to find out how true blue you really are.

1 **You're playing Monopoly and you have a chance to get ahead on the board. The only problem: You have to cheat to do it. What do you do?**

a) No cheating, no matter what. You play the game honestly.

b) Maybe if you try to move on the sly—no one will notice.

c) Go ahead and cheat. How else are you going to win?

"Let's go to a movie!"

"Let's have a party!"

"LET'S STUDY!"

"Let's play tennis!"

2 You and your friends can't agree on what to do on Saturday afternoon. Everyone has different ideas. How do you resolve the situation?

a) Stay low key and let your friends decide what to do.

b) Suggest going to a place where everyone might have fun, like a supermall.

c) Tell your friends that you need to do it your way—or else.

3 You just caught your friend telling a lie to her parents. What do you say?

a) After her parents go, confront your friend about the lie.

b) Ignore the lie. She won't do it again.

c) Tell your friend's mom everything, even if it means making your friend mad.

4 Your best friend's parents are going through a rough divorce. How can you help?

a) Listen.

b) Offer your own advice.

c) Tell your friend to get over it.

5 You find a wallet with a thousand dollars in cash inside it. What do you do?

    a) Find the address and/or name in the wallet and return it.

    b) Take $100 out of the wallet as a finder's fee and then call the owner.

    c) Pocket the wallet and don't bother to call anyone.

6 You're in the middle of a nature trail when someone approaches you and tells you she's lost. She asks for your help. What do you do?

    a) Take out your map and compass and offer to walk with her until she gets her bearings.

    b) Point her on the path marked THIS WAY and hope she'll figure it out.

    c) Tell her you can't help and walk away.

7 Someone walks up to you on the street, thinking you're a famous movie star. How do you act?

    a) You politely shake your head and whisper, "Aw, you've got me mixed up with someone else, but thanks."

b) You laugh and toss your head back while pretending to be famous for fifteen minutes, even though you're not.

c) You smile broadly, thank the fan, and start signing books with the star's name.

8 **Your little brother embarrasses you in front of all your friends. You have this reaction. . . .**

a) You can't stop giggling, and you can't shake the blush on your cheeks.

b) You think of a great comeback that gets all your friends laughing. You can take a joke, especially when you make a nice recovery.

c) Now it's your turn to tease your little brother. It's payback time!

Answers

. . . .

Mostly As = BIG Heart.
You feel things deeply all the time. Your first instinct in any situation is to give someone a big squeeze and tell them you love 'em. People depend on you for your kindness and generosity.

. . . .

Mostly *B*s = BIG Ears.

You've always got an ear to the ground—listening for clues and cues about what people are doing and saying. You like to try new things, but usually you won't do anything too risky. You don't like conflict or confrontation, but make sure you're not compromising too much trying not to rock the boat.

Mostly *C*s = BIG Mouth.

You aren't exactly a steel trap when it comes to keeping secrets, so don't be surprised if your friends don't always confide in you. And sometimes you choose the easiest path instead of the straight and narrow one. Be careful you're not putting your own needs before your friends'. You are, however, a lot of fun. You do things over-the-top and always get a lot of attention for it.

Box O' Compliments

USUALLY WHEN LIBBY, SAM, AND RACHEL ARE FEELING BLUE
(AND EVEN WHEN THEY AREN'T), I LIKE TO GIVE THEM A SPECIAL
COMPLIMENT. THEY ALWAYS SAY IT BRIGHTENS THEIR DAY.
TRY SOME OF THESE OUT ON YOUR FRIENDS!

I am so lucky to have a friend like you.

You look fabulous today.

Thanks for always thinking of me.

You are sooooo talented. Way to go!

I didn't know you looked so good in (color she's wearing).

I love that (shirt/sweater/jacket) you're wearing.

You are one of the most talented peeps I know.

Can I borrow that (item) sometime? It's so cool.

You are one of the smartest people I know.

Is there something different about your hair? I love it!

Rate What You ATE

Remember that eating smart is good. The healthier you eat, the better you'll feel and the more energy you'll have. But don't forget, exercise is just as important! My mom always told me that the key to life is taking the stairs and not the elevator. In other words, don't just sit there. Move to the groove. Yeah!

What's the better food for your lunch box?

1 Grilled chicken on a roll **OR** Chicken fingers?

2 Chocolate milk **OR** Diet soda?

3 Candy bar **OR** Peanuts and raisins?

4 Banana chips **OR** Potato chips?

5 Fruit roll-up **OR** French fries?

6 Orange **OR** Banana?

Answers:

1. Choose the grilled chicken instead of the chicken fingers. 2. Grilled is better than fried. 3. Try not to pick soda of any kind. Milk is a better bet—even with chocolate. 3. Nuts and raisins. 4. Banana chips, all the way! They taste yummier, too. 5. Fruit roll-up, definitely. 6. Oranges and bananas are both good for you (and yes, that was a trick question).

More Healthy Snack Ideas 4 U

1. Carrots and celery dipped in low-fat ranch dressing

2. Dry cereal mixed with plain yogurt

3. Nuts like peanuts, almonds, or pecans mixed with raisins

4. Frozen orange juice ice cubes (or any 100 percent juice blend)

5. Peanut butter spread on sliced apple

6. Air-popped popcorn

Are you a brainiac or a supergirl?

Are you the life of the party, or do you like to play it safe? Rate Your PQ, or Personality Quotient, with these simple questions.

1 **What shape necklace would you pick?**

a) ♥

c) ☺

b) #1

d) ⚡

2 **What color do you love?**

a) Deep purple

b) Shocking pink

c) Sunny yellow

d) Dark brown

3 **What sound do you like the best?**

   a) Classical music

   b) Fireworks

   c) Ice-cream truck

   d) Whistling wind

4 **What makes you happiest?**

   a) Hanging out in a bookstore

   b) Winning a contest

   c) Making people laugh

   d) Watching a favorite TV show

5 **Which of these features is your favorite?**

   a) Eyes

   b) Mouth

   c) Nose

   d) Feet

6 **Which of these is most like your role in your group?**

   a) Planner

   b) Leader

   c) Idea person

   d) Silent partner

7 When you're sad, you're most likely to:

a) Pull out your handkerchief and sniffle.

b) Start bawling.

c) Make a joke instead of crying.

d) Stop speaking and get really quiet.

8 When you sleep, you:

a) Have sweet dreams.

b) Wake in fits and starts.

c) Can never fall asleep in the first place!

d) Snooze like a rock.

9 What do you do with your money?

a) Save it.

b) Spend it.

c) Give it away.

d) Hide it.

10 Do you believe in ghosts?

a) No way. Show me proof.

b) I believe in lots of magical things. Why not?

c) Why, there's a ghost in my bedroom right now!

d) Don't even say the word *ghost*! Just thinking about it keeps me awake at night.

11 **When you are superexcited, you're most likely to:**

a) Clap your hands together.

b) Throw a party for your best pals.

c) Jump up and down and do a flip in the air (if you know how).

d) Cross your fingers that the good times last.

Answers:

If you chose mostly *As*, you're a BRAINIAC.
You like to read, write in your journal, prove scientific theorems, and talk about your feelings (in a deep and meaningful way, of course). Sometimes other friends don't totally get you because they don't think about stuff as much as you do. Although it's important to remember that sometimes not everything has to be so serious, you're doing great. Your practical view of the world serves you very well. Keep up the good work!

If you chose mostly *Bs*, you're a SUPERGIRL.
Juggling sports, the school play, and a cooking class—plus homework, laps around the track, and feeding your cat? No problem! You were born to multitask. In fact, you do everything with a flourish. Now your closet may not always be superneat, but that doesn't matter when you're conquering the world in your spare time. Your middle name is "winner" and others love to follow your lead.

If you chose mostly *C*s, you're the LIFE OF THE PARTY.

Goofing around is second nature to you. Thank goodness! Your friends love to laugh and play around. It helps that you don't always take yourself too seriously—so you're a little more accessible than some of your more intense pals. Although you like to crack up, it doesn't always mean that you're goofing off. Sometimes your label of "silly" just means that you know how to have a great time.

If you chose mostly *D*s, you PLAY IT SAFE.

Sometimes you let your imagination get the better of you. Although you tend to get good grades and great support from friends and family, you're always looking over your shoulder to see if something not-so-great is coming down the road. Just remember that being too scared of stuff means you might not have a chance to enjoy yourself as much. And isn't life too short not to take chances now and then?

Are You Really in Your ELEMENT?

Are you Air, Water, Fire, or Earth? Which of the four elements matches your personality? Take this quiz to find out!

Is it hot in here? No? Hmmph. That's funny, because I feel an itsy-bitsy bit warm. . . .

MY BUDS SAY I'M DOWN-TO-EARTH. SO, I GUESS THIS LABEL MAKES SENSE—EVEN THOUGH I SECRETLY HATE LABELS.

Check this out! I'm not just water—
I'm ice, rain, and dew. There are sooo
many sides to me.

When I think of elements, I think of high
wind, sleet, and earthquakes. Sort of
like a bad day at school.

1 **If you were a crayon, you'd be . . .**

    a) Fire-engine red

    (b)) Cloudy blue

    c) Seaweed green

    d) Mossy brown

2 **Where would you feel most at home?**

    a) Lounging on a beach somewhere.

    b) Falling asleep in a hammock.

    c) Sitting next to a stream.

    d) Planting flowers in the backyard.

3 **What do you like more?**

    a) Curried chicken

    b) Popcorn with light butter

    c) Sundae with whipped cream

    d) Peanut butter crackers

4 **Of these adjectives, the one that describes you best is . . .**

    a) Sassy

    b) Chilled out

    c) Emotional

    d) Strong

5 **What are you most likely to do when you're alone?**

a) Plan my class president acceptance speech.

b) Send e-mails to all my friends.

c) Make a collage for my grandmother.

d) Clean my room.

6 **What quality do you most look for in a friend?**

a) Sense of humor

b) Thoughtfulness

c) Creativity

d) Dependability

7 **What would you most likely do to vent your anger?**

a) Scream at the top of my lungs.

b) I don't get angry very much.

c) Punch a pillow until I feel better.

d) Go for a long walk around the block.

8 **What is your favorite season?**

a) Summer

b) Spring

c) Autumn

d) Winter

9 **What smell do you like the best?**

    a) BBQ grill

    b) Rain

    c) Perfumed lotion

    d) Flowers

10 **Which of these is the best kind of movie snack?**

    a) Nachos

    b) Popcorn

    c) Twizzlers

    d) Milk Duds

11 **Where would you go first if you were given a free vacation?**

    a) Greek Islands

    b) Mount Everest

    c) Great Barrier Reef

    d) Grand Canyon

12 **What kind of music is currently in your CD player or iPod?**

    a) New wave or punk

    b) Top 40

    c) Folk

    d) Rock and roll

How Did You Do?

You got mostly *As*, so your primary element is . . .

FIRE

You blaze hot. You're always embracing someone or something. You are extremely creative and full of life. Sometimes you can be a little bit bossy and opinionated, but that's cool. You're a strong individual. People look to you for leadership.

You got mostly *Bs*, so your primary element is . . .

AIR

You have a good deal of balance in all things. You're a super communicator, which makes you an excellent friend. You have a natural curiosity, and you're great at staying cool, calm, and collected even when things get stressful. One of your favorite things to do is help others.

You got mostly *C*s, so your primary element is . . .

WATER

You're very emotional—but in a good way. You have an intuitive nature and your sense of compassion makes you sensitive to other people's needs, fears, and talents. You tend to be a big dreamer, which gives you an idealistic outlook on the world and the people in it. You are the best listener among your friends.

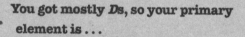

You got mostly *D*s, so your primary element is . . .

EARTH

Like the earth below your feet, you are totally grounded. You like to build things from the bottom up. Among your friends, you're typically the responsible and dependable one. You use your practical smarts to solve problems.

This or That?

Take the test on your own. Then test a friend. How many of your answers are the same?

Half-empty **OR** Half-full

Deep thinker **OR** Space case

Dance **OR** Yoga

Class president **OR** Class clown

Secrets **OR** Gossip

Summer **OR** Winter

Cinnamon **OR** Peppermint

Scream **OR** Whisper

Socks **OR** Barefoot

Hot chocolate **OR** Herbal tea

Bling **OR** Nothing

Rain **OR** Snow

Head **OR** Heart

Hoodie **OR** Sweater

Staples **OR** Tape

Take-out **OR** Homemade

Mope **OR** Cope

Sunrise **OR** Sunset

Pop **OR** Rock

Can't We All Just Get Along?

Laugh.

I feel good about myself and my friends when everyone is having a good time. Sometimes I read books of jokes just so I have one ready to go when the mood strikes.

LISTEN.

THE ONLY WAY A FRIENDSHIP TRULY SUCCEEDS IS IF EVERYONE LISTENS TO EVERYONE ELSE. SOMETIMES WE'RE ALL SO BUSY TRYING TO MAKE A POINT THAT WE DON'T SEE WHEN OUR FRIENDS NEED US MOST.

Play fair.

Here's what I've learned about the true meaning of friendship: You cannot lie. The best part about all of my friends is that they love and accept me. But that's because no matter what else happens, I always try to be honest. I trust them, and they trust me.

Deal.

Everyone is allowed a bad day. Okay, maybe even two or more bad days. But our job as one another's friends is to just deal with it. The key to friendship is acceptance. My friends accept me with quirks and all. I love them for that.

Are You a Friend 4-Ever?

For the questions on this quiz, scribble the answers you think for your-self and a friend. Or, have your friend answer along with you. You can always add more lines for more answers if other friends want to play, too.

1. After a really bad day, what cheers you up the most?

you: _____

friend: _____

2. What outfit would you wear to the first day of school?

you: _____

friend: _____

3. It's a snow day. What do you do?

you: _____

friend: _____

4. What is your ideal pet?

you: _____

friend: _____

5. What would you wear to the school dance?

you: _____

friend: _____

6. If you have extra time in school, what do you do?

you: _____

friend: _____

7. What's your favorite thing in the fridge?

you: _____

friend: _____

8. What's inside your backpack?

you: _____

friend: _____

Now that you have filled in all of the blanks, try to figure out which of the Friends 4-Ever girls you are the most like. Are you and your friends a perfect mix of all types—or do you have a clique of Rachels or Sams? Have fun figuring it out. . . .

Are you JESSIE? Smart, secure, friendly, and the number-one reader during your library's summer reading program.

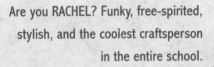

Are you RACHEL? Funky, free-spirited, stylish, and the coolest craftsperson in the entire school.

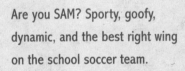

Are you SAM? Sporty, goofy, dynamic, and the best right wing on the school soccer team.

Are you LIBBY? Glammerific, outgoing, fresh, and the number-one school volunteer three years in a row.

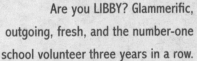

Now the quizzes are over and done . . .
But the best part of friendship has only begun!

Here's hoping you and your friends will stay together
4-ever . . . just like us!

c u soon!

Samantha Rachel Jessie Libby